the john ritchie

family series

let's talk about THE UNEQUAL YOKE

1

JOHN RITCHIE LTD
CHRISTIAN PUBLICATIONS

Copyright © 2008 John Ritchie Ltd., 40 Beansburn, Kilmarnock, Scotland

ISBN-13: 978 0 946351 71 8

ISBN-10: 0 946351 71 6

Typeset & Print: John Ritchie Ltd., 40 Beansburn, Kilmarnock, KA3 1RH

www.ritchiechristianmedia.co.uk   email: sales@johnritchie.co.uk

Illustrations: J. Glen

Contents

Introduction

He had such a good background. When he came to live in their city the people could see that he was a man to be trusted, and that was rare enough in their society. As he looked around, this appeared to be an ideal place to put down his roots, much more attractive and promising than the place he had left. Certainly there were features of his fellow citizens which he found distasteful, but this was balanced by the attractiveness of the area and the thrill and excitement of the life of the city. His wife and family settled in well and he quickly made his presence felt. He prospered, and over the years became a prominent citizen, eventually being appointed to the position of magistrate. Everything seemed to be going so well for his household. From outward appearances there was nothing lacking and the move which he had made into the area had brought only prosperity.

What, however, the people of the town did not realise was that this man's heart was consumed with grief as he looked at the conditions around him. The violence, immorality, and godlessness which he encountered daily vexed him, all the more so as he thought of earlier days when things had been so different. He looked back to times when he had kept company with godly people and when, in the home of his uncle, he had enjoyed being close to a man of God. Perhaps with regret he remembered the decision he had taken to leave his uncle and to set up home in this locality, but he could not go back, so close were the links which he had forged with the men and women of the city. His daughters had married into local families and his whole life was now centred on Sodom. His name was Lot.

What a sad picture Lot presents to us. He had become unequally yoked together with unbelievers, and a life which had shown so much promise in its youth is now powerless in the service of God. Domestically and commercially he had taken unequal yokes upon his shoulders, initially enjoying some of the fame and fortune which these brought. But enjoyment was diminishing and he was finding that increasingly the dark shadow of vexation was taking its place.

Lot's powerlessness really became evident when the day of reckoning came. Two visitors brought him news of the impending judgement of God on the city, and made it clear that he and his family had to flee. But they were very reluctant to go.

What lessons do we learn from the sad experience of this man whose life promised so much? Firstly we see that establishing close links with the men of the world did not increase their regard for him. Maybe he thought he could influence events in Sodom for good; but the men of that city pursued their own course in spite of him. He was not able to improve the standards of behaviour of society. Even when he tried to keep his visitors safe from the mob at his door who wished to get at them, the scant respect the men of Sodom had for him became all too clear.

Beware of the dangers of close associations with unbelievers!

Also we learn that his family had little respect for him. We know that he had a wife, at least two married daughters, no fewer than two sons, and possibly two unmarried daughters. Yet only two of his daughters escaped with him from Sodom. What a price to pay for befriending the world!

You will find this story in Genesis chapters 13 and 19. When we see Lot for the last time he is in a state of intoxication, indulging insensibly in lewd acts. He has lost all he had and all he tried to build in Sodom.

How did a life which had such a promising start descend to such depths? The answer is that he acquired a love for the world and, as a result, he and his loved ones became unequally yoked together with unbelievers.

Beware of the dangers of close associations with unbelievers! So vital are the issues that it is important to understand what the Bible has to teach on this matter.

The unequal yoke today

In the complex, modern society in which we live, the Christian is faced with a multitude of decisions when considering marriage, employment, spare-time interests, and bringing up a family. The issues in many of these decisions can be difficult and there are times when the way ahead is not too clearly discernible. But one of the basic considerations to be taken into account when we have to decide our course in life is the question of the unequal yoke.

The view of young believers

Young believers often look at the life of their parents and other older believers and consider it to be too restricted and narrow. The range of friends which they have and the interests which occupy their time seems to be so limited and because of this they would appear to be missing out on so much in life.

There is a danger that those who are brought up in a christian home do not fully understand the differences which exist between Christians and others. Any line of demarcation and separation from the world can be seen to be nothing but old-fashioned narrow thinking which takes much of the enjoyment out of life. Some families may be prepared to admit that the mode of life adopted by their parents is fine for that older generation, but say that things have changed now, and the youth of today have opportunities which their parents never enjoyed - therefore our attitude to our relationships with others must surely be different?

This attitude fails to appreciate that the life which is separate from the world is not a dull, narrow, grey existence. Rather it is the best kind of life, and one which gives an enjoyment the unbeliever knows nothing about.

Also there may be a feeling that this 'old-fashioned' life-style limits effective witness in the work of the gospel. It is true that the life of the spiritual isolationist makes gospel witness most difficult, but biblical separation does not mean a life of isolation nor does it encourage that.

When vital decisions in life are taken without appreciating the biblical truth of separation, it is possible to start on a pathway which will limit your usefulness in the service of God and which will cause you bitter regrets in later years.

> Biblical separation does not mean a life of isolation

The danger to older believers

Neglect of this truth is not, however, confined to those who are younger. Many Christians who are more mature find that their sense of separation from the world changes with the passing years. The pressures and problems of life can erode our desire to steer clear of links with the world. The opportunity for gain and the perceived 'benefits' of worldly ties can distort our view of the unequal yoke. When we do now what we never would have done in our earlier years, we excuse it as the extremism of youth in contrast to the more mature pathway which we now travel. But is it?

To look more closely at the issues involved we must ask the leading question: what do we mean when we speak about the unequal yoke? Let us look at what the Scriptures teach.

The teaching of the Bible

"Be ye not unequally yoked together with unbelievers"
(2 Cor 6:14).

To be yoked together is to be joined together in a common purpose which so limits your freedom of action that you can act only with the approval of the one to whom you are yoked.

The initial picture which comes to mind is of two animals, probably oxen, yoked together ploughing a field. They are

engaged in
a common purpose
and their freedom is restricted,
because each beast can only move with the agreement of the other. The benefit of the yoke, of course, is that the two can accomplish together what they could not accomplish if they worked separately. Co-operation in a common task is the very essence of the yoke, and there is no doubt that this can be an attractive approach to many of the tasks which we have to tackle.

There are limits beyond which a Christian must not go

But Paul is warning us that there are limits beyond which a Christian must not go. We must never yoke ourselves together with those who are unbelievers. We must not engage with them in a common purpose which restricts our freedom and makes it possible for us to do only that of which they approve. The priority of the

Christian is the honour of the Lord Jesus but this is never in the mind of the unbeliever. Such a yoke will inevitably lead to compromise.

Note the five-fold basis of the appeal in 2 Corinthians 6:14-16.

1.   What fellowship hath righteousness with unrighteousess?

What participation can righteousness have with unrighteousness? An unbeliever is the servant of sin and a believer is the servant of righteousness. These two are opposed to each other. In an unequal yoke there is one partner who is concerned with dealing in a righteous, God-honouring way, whereas the other has no such concerns and is prepared to engage in methods of which the believer cannot approve.

2.   What communion hath light with darkness?

The word 'communion' here means fellowship, to have a common mind. Light and darkness are mutually exclusive. It is not possible to have both together. One of the first creative acts of God was to separate light and darkness. As light and darkness cannot mix neither can believers and unbelievers. There can be no agreement of mind between them.

How can two agree when their lives have opposite foundations?

3.   What concord hath Christ with Belial?

What possible agreement can there be between Christ and Belial? This is the only occasion in the New Testament when the word Belial is used and it refers to Satan. To have concord is to have complete harmony and it is impossible for a follower of the Lord Jesus to be in complete harmony with one who is under the power of Satan. The unbeliever will not consider the spiritual well-being of his partner when decisions have to be taken.

4.   What part hath he that believeth with an infidel?

How can these two people have part or share anything together? The infidel is an unbeliever. One believes God and trusts in His word but the other does not believe God and has no faith in Him. How can two agree when their lives have such opposite foundations?

5.   *What agreement hath the temple of God with idols?*

The temple of God is where the holiness of God is maintained, the other is where God is dishonoured. How can there be any common opinion or any common views? The practice of idolatry is completely opposed to all that the Christian believes, therefore there can be no coming together of minds between these two.

In such a forceful way, therefore, we have been shown how impossible it is to be unequally yoked together with an unbeliever and to find peace and benefit in the association. The differences which exist are not of our invention. They are not attitudes which Christians drift into because they do not mix much with unbelievers. They are not the product of spiritual pride. These are differences which God has made.

the differences
enable believers
to enjoy God to
the full

If you are feeling that this teaching is very negative and restricting, you must remember that the differences between believers and unbelievers have not been made to restrict the life of the Christian and to turn it into a monotonous existence. They rather enable believers to enjoy God to the full. Relationships with those who are not Christians are to be restricted so that an unequal yoke is avoided. But what is that compared to the glorious relationship between God the Father and those who have put their trust in Him? That is why we are told to "come out from among them, and be ye separate" (2 Cor 6:17). As in every aspect of life, what God asks us to do is for our blessing, and any alternative, no matter how attractive, is unprofitable and potentially disastrous.

The unequal yoke in marriage

The closest relationship into which a man and a woman enters is marriage. In view of the teaching of Scripture on the subject of the unequal yoke it is clear that it is not the will of God that a believer and an unbeliever should marry. This is confirmed by Paul's insistence that marriage must be only "in the Lord" (1 Cor 7:39). Why is it, therefore, that some believers enter into a marriage with an unbeliever, and what problems does this cause?

Marrying an unbeliever

It is very easy for a young man or woman to let their feelings take control of their lives and to neglect the teaching of Scripture. A young believer may meet someone and begin to feel the pull of physical attraction. You feel that your friend has a life-style which is so different from what you have known and this adds to the attraction.

marriage must be only "in the Lord"

As you get to know each other better you find that this life style is one which is 'respectable' and does not include the extremes of sin. He or she never uses bad language, rarely spends their leisure time in places which are offensive to you, and is known to be honourable and upright. You may even find that when you explain that you are a Christian and regularly attend the gatherings of the assembly, there is no opposition to this. Indeed you may even be encouraged to continue to go, because it means so much to you. What then can be wrong with marrying someone as nice and reasonable as this? You can continue with your christian life, which, you hope, may even be helpful in bringing your new husband or wife to a knowledge of salvation.

After all the issues have been considered, marriage to an unbeliever comes about because the Christian finds this attraction to be greater than the attraction of obeying the word of God. It is

11

therefore evidence of a heart which is not close to the Lord and is prepared to openly disobey the Scriptures.

Marriage to any unbeliever is forbidden in Scripture

It is rare, although not unknown, to find a believer marrying an unbeliever whose manner of life is openly sinful and who shows utter contempt for the gospel. For most Christians this would be just too much to take. Remember, however, that it is not marriage to certain types of unbelievers which is forbidden; marriage to any unbeliever is forbidden in Scripture. Marrying someone who appears to have all the attributes you would desire, apart from the fact that they do not possess salvation is a very real danger.

The problems encountered

The problem of the foundations of home life.

The first problem which is faced is the foundation on which you will build your life together. As a believer you will wish to put the Lord Jesus first in every area of your life. As a wife you will wish your husband to be the head of the home, and as a husband you will wish your wife to acknowledge that you are the head of the home. Right at the beginning you are faced with the fact that the unbeliever knows nothing of these truths and has no wish to put them into practice. The unbelieving partner will want to build home-life according to the principles and practice of this present age. In the early stage of marriage these issues may not seem to be important, and the novelty and excitement of being together may put out of your mind any first stirrings of anxiety. As time passes, however, the issues will assume greater importance and you will realise that the very foundations of the marriage are unsound. Every major decision will reveal the gulf which exists between you. "Can two walk together, except they be agreed?" is the question of Amos 3:3. You will quickly learn the answer!

The problem of interests

This is one area where the differences will be very clear. Can you be happy living with a marriage partner who shares few of your interests? Can you be content knowing that you share little of your partner's interests? Your husband wishes to go to places of entertainment which you do not wish to frequent. Your wife does not accompany you to the gatherings of the assembly. How can you possibly reconcile such different outlooks on life? Gradually you will find that you are each living different lives. Most husbands and wives are apart during working hours, but to spend your leisure hours apart is not beneficial to any marriage. Married life involves sharing everything, but in the unequal yoke there are large areas which cannot be shared. This adds greatly to the strain of life together.

There are large areas which cannot be shared

The problem of bringing up children

When children come along the believer will wish to bring them up in an atmosphere which is honouring to the Lord Jesus. When the child is very young this may not seem to be a major issue, but as the years pass, like other problems, it becomes greater. An unbelieving father may wish to take the child to places which his wife does not find acceptable. An unbelieving mother may resent the fact that the children are being taught Scripture. Some compromise may be reached but the child will grow up realising that there is a fundamental difference in the home. There can be no united testimony before the child's eyes.

The problems of bringing up a family are great enough without these added difficulties. Children need clear instruction and teaching, and this cannot be given to them when mother and father have no agreement on important spiritual issues. The pain of seeing children drifting into the world is great enough for a believer, without having to face up to the fact that this drift was helped by the influence of an unbelieving parent.

The problem of facing eternity.

In the early years of marriage this may be another of these questions which you can put to the back of your mind. Life stretches before you with all its promise and, although you are married to an unbeliever, you hope that salvation will come and that both of you one day will be united in this. It may be that you do not care presently about these matters. Life has to be lived and enjoyed today.

Gradually, however, as the years pass, thoughts will enter your mind in quiet moments. You are going to be with the Lord, but you are sharing your life with one who is not, and eternal separation lies ahead of you. Remember that there is no promise in Scripture that an unsaved husband or wife will be saved. By the grace of God this may be so, but it is not promised. You keep banishing this from your mind, but it will not stay away, so you satisfy yourself with some woolly thought that the Lord will take care of everything and that such a good loving husband or wife must surely belong to the Lord. But you know deep down that you are ignoring Scripture, just as you ignored it when you married!

You know deep down that you are ignoring Scripture

The problem of maintaining your spiritual life

There is no doubt that to deliberately marry an unbeliever is an act of disobedience to the Lord and to the Scriptures. It is evidence of the fact that you are away in heart from the Lord. You may protest that this is not so, and that you intend continuing with an interest in spiritual matters, but consider for a moment the difficulties which you face.

In the home the word of God must be read daily and there must be a time of prayer. An unbelieving husband cannot take the lead in this, and an unbelieving wife cannot participate. At the beginning there may be some attempt to do so but time will soon erode any determination to continue. How can it be otherwise? Those who do not have the Lord Jesus as their Saviour cannot be expected to have an interest in daily prayer and Scripture reading.

Outside of the home the Christian enjoys the fellowship of other Christians, but this kind of company cannot be enjoyable to those who do not know the Saviour. You attend the gatherings of the assembly as best you can, but you do so alone. You may go together for some time, but this will not be sustained.

Difficulties also occur when entertaining other Christians in your home. The unbelieving partner will find it very difficult to engage in conversation with those whose interests and way of life are so different from what he or she knows. Your home cannot be open to other Christians for fellowship as you would like.

The overall effect

Marriage to an unbeliever has many problems

Marriage, therefore, to an unbeliever has many problems. It leads to the believer dividing life into two separate compartments, home life and assembly life. It will lead to two different sets of friends, and to attempting to balance two different sets of values.

What if I am married to an unbeliever?

Once you are married you cannot change that fact. Marriage to an unbeliever is forbidden, but once marriage takes place, in the eyes of Lord you are married. You can take a number of approaches to live with the problem.

The first approach is to determine to continue with your spiritual life no matter what strain this puts you under. Your partner may be happy for you to do so, because he or she will regard this merely as 'church membership' and will see little point in arguing over which 'church' you attend. If you sustain your spiritual life and read the Bible regularly, there will soon dawn on your soul what a mistake you have made. There may even be resentment that there is a side to your life which you do not share with your partner. You will learn by bitter experience how restrictive is marriage to an unbeliever. This will produce regrets which you will harbour in your heart, for they cannot be discussed with the one you have married.

The second, opposite approach is to allow your spiritual life to go. This may be due to the opposition to spiritual things which a previously indifferent partner now displays, or it may be simply due to the fact that without any encouragement in the home your interest slowly wanes.

One other situation is often seen, and you must consider this carefully. If at the time of marriage, you were backslidden and caring little for the effect of the unequal yoke, you may find that the early of years of marriage have few of the problems to which we have referred, because you have been happy to go along with the life-style of your unbelieving husband or wife. When a family comes along, however, or simply with the passing years, things start to change. As you consider the future of your children you realise that they need the teaching which you received as a child, and that they need christian guidance. A mother, for example, starts to take her children to Sunday School, and meeting other Christians at that time, she enjoys their company and her heart stirs again towards spiritual matters. She feels that standards at home must be an example to the children. Her husband, however, becomes confused, and cannot understand why matters which were of so little interest to her when they were courting and in the early years of marriage, suddenly became important. He maintains that she has changed, and may feel resentment, as we have already seen, that she is building a side to her life in which he plays no part. He may feel that the Bible is causing a division in his home.

No matter how you tackle the problems there will always have to be an element of compromise. A wife cannot always say no to her husband when he wishes her to accompany him to functions etc. A husband cannot cut himself off from great areas of his wife's life.

You may compromise by attending a 'church' where the unbeliever is received and to which he or she is prepared to go. Compromise may be necessary in what you allow into your home, or in the 'friends' with whom you spend your time. None of this is for your spiritual good.

The sad fact is that you, as a Christian, can never look back and blame this situation on the unbeliever. They did not know the Scriptures, and they had no knowledge whatsoever of the teaching regarding the unequal yoke. You, on the other hand, did know. You may well have been warned by those who had a care for you, but you went ahead, disregarding the spiritual advice which you received. Your feelings were so strong that you felt that everything would work out well at the end of the day. Someone as mannerly, good-living and caring as your fiancee would make an ideal life partner, and if the Lord had allowed you to fall in love, He would ensure that your fiancee will come to know the Saviour. That was how you reasoned, but it has not turned out that way. Living together has thrown into stark relief the fundamental differences between you. This is your responsibility alone. You turned your back on the word of God, and too late you found that the truth of Bible teaching works out in your lives. You are living in the atmosphere of 'what might have been'.

What you must do nevertheless is continue to pray and work for the salvation of your partner. Show a good testimony in the home without making every day an opportunity for a sermon. To see you both united in acknowledging that Jesus Christ is Lord is a goal towards which it is worth striving.

> There are fundamental differences between you

> Continue to pray and work for the salvation of your partner

Salvation after marriage

As we have seen, it is contrary to Scripture for a believer to marry an unbeliever, but when after marriage a husband or wife accepts the Lord Jesus as Saviour, they are presented with the problem of living with one who does not share their faith. Scripture is quite clear that salvation does not annul the marriage bond. In 1 Corinthians 7:12-13 we read, "If any brother hath a wife that believeth not, and she be pleased to dwell with him, let him not put her away. And the woman which hath a husband that believeth not, and if he be pleased to dwell with her, let her not leave him." We cannot argue that after salvation we are a new creation and therefore all relationships have changed. The marriage bond continues after the spiritual change has taken place, and if the unbeliever is willing to remain with a husband or wife who is now a changed person, they should continue to live together as husband and wife.

Show great wisdom and tact in testifying in the home

The new situation - a believer in the family

When a husband or wife suddenly finds this new situation of having a believer in the family they will be confused, perhaps antagonistic, and certainly rather afraid of all that is involved. In our present day there will be the fear that some sect or strange cult has taken over, and that destruction of the marriage is inevitable. The believer has to show great wisdom and tact in testifying in the home. It will not be wise to commence preaching constantly to unbelieving members of the family. This will weary them and cause severe strains on the relationship. On the other hand it would not be faithful to the Lord for you to continue as if no change had taken place. There may, for instance, have been places to which you went in the past, but which your conscience will not now allow you to enter, although your unbelieving partner wishes you to continue with that mode of life.

18

This is where real difficulties can occur which have to be handled with tact and patience. The believer must explain the change which has taken place in their life and what they will not now be free to do. If, for example, you are a believing wife whose husband insists that you obey him, there must be prayerful consideration of the issues involved. On some occasions you may feel that although what he is asking would not be your choice, you are compromising no truth nor dishonouring the Lord by doing as he asks. On the other hand you may feel that it is not possible to do his bidding, but do not seek confrontation on the matter. Explain your views, and above all continue to be a loving wife. Indeed it is a good testimony for your husband to see that you are now a better wife due to salvation having come into your life.

Do not seek confrontation

Testimony in the home

"...that, if any obey not the word, they also may without the word be won by the conversation of the wives" (1 Peter 3:1).

Peter's advice here to wives with unbelieving husbands applies equally to husbands with unbelieving wives. Do not weary the unbeliever by constantly lecturing them, turning every conversation round until the gospel is brought in. This will cause resentment, even although your motive is a desire to see them saved. The result of this will be that the gospel is a subject which always causes disagreement in the home. When opportunities occur however, you should take them and speak of the gospel quietly and in a controlled way. It is not helpful to become shrill and over dramatic in what you say.

Peter was a married man and understood married life. He advises you to be a living sermon in the home so that without a word being spoken there is conviction of sin brought into the hearts of those who are close to you. A changed life may at times cause frustration and anger to others in the home, but when the positive and beneficial nature of the change is seen, it commends the gospel. Let it be clear that salvation has not diminished your love, rather that Scripture put

Be a living sermon in the home

into practice makes your home a happier place. This will not always be easy to carry out. There will be times when remarks are made which make you angry, but keep a clear head and remember that little prayers for help can be offered up even when you are busy about the house.

As a result of behaving like this your unbelieving partner is not faced with daily doses of sermons. What is seen, however, is something much more powerful. He is looking constantly at a living sermon in the home. Daily before his eyes the teaching of the Bible is being lived out.

The purpose of living like this is to see your partner and family saved, and a good testimony before them is a solid foundation on which to work. Do not become extreme, outrageous or completely unreasonable in your demands. Be slow to anger and always remember that you may be the only example of a Christian ever seen by your loved ones. They will judge your salvation, and the Bible, by what they see in you. In 1 Corinthians 7:14 Paul tells us that the unbelieving husband is sanctified by the wife, the unbelieving wife is sanctified by the husband and the children are holy. This means that they are set apart for the imparting of godly influence, not that they are saved by the presence of a believer in the home. It is your responsibility as a Christian to ensure that this godly influence is strongly felt.

If the unbelieving depart

In some cases unbelievers are not prepared to live with believers, and despite all attempts to prevent them going, they decide to leave the home. Paul writes of this in 1 Corinthians 7:15, "But if the unbelieving depart, let them depart. A brother or a sister is not under bondage in such cases; but God hath called us to peace."

No one can doubt the sadness which this course of action can create, but the Lord will give comfort and support to all who have to pass through these circumstances for the sake of the gospel. He will not allow His child to be overwhelmed in this storm. The believer is not under bondage to continue with one who does not wish their presence and who may well make life difficult, if not unbearable, and who is no longer prepared to live as husband or wife. God has called us in peace and we do not need to return to a life where there is no peace in the home. There is no allowance here to remarry while the departed husband or wife is still alive, but the One who took you through these difficult days will continue to support you for as long as is necessary.

God has called us in peace

The unequal yoke in business

It is not only in the home that the question of the unequal yoke has to be faced. There are often great temptations at work to enter into agreements which are financially beneficial, but which involve compromise.

Employees

Let us be quite clear that when an ordinary employee is working for a company or even for an individual, this is not being linked in an unequal yoke. Such an employee has an agreement with the employer to work a certain number of hours per week or month and is paid an agreed sum of money.

There are examples of such employees in Scripture. Erastus was the chamberlain of the city, possibly the city of Corinth (Rom 16:23). He was a local government official of some standing and seniority. When Paul was at Philippi he was imprisoned, and after the earthquake which released him, the jailor and his family believed the gospel. Paul gave no instruction to this man to leave his employment. There is clear teaching in the New Testament that servants must count their masters worthy of all honour, that the name of God and His doctrine be not blasphemed (1 Tim 6:1).

Servants must count their masters worthy of all honour

There is nothing to suggest that Erastus should leave his job, or that christian servants should seek to leave their masters. Thus employees such as Erastus and the Philippian jailer are not regarded as being in an unequal yoke.

Partners in business

What then constitutes an unequal yoke in business? Being

party to a partnership agreement is very different from being an employee. As a partner you are bound to the agreements into which the partnership enters and you have no freedom of action once these are in force. It may be that you would argue against certain agreements, but the majority in the partnership will always carry the matter through. The relationship between partners in a business is much closer than that which exists between employee and employer.

The difference between this and an ordinary employer/employee relationship is that in a partnership you are personally party to all agreements and decisions which are made in the running of the business. You can see that this could cause serious difficulties. There are many unbelievers who act with integrity and honesty, but even with such upright individuals there will be issues where the believer could not support all that is done, and this will cause conflict. Where the partners do not have such standards of integrity and honesty the pitfalls are more plain to see.

This can be a particularly difficult problem for those who are engaged in types of employment where partnerships are the accepted method of organising business. A young believer can be faced with the prospect of joining an organisation, knowing that progress in his profession will take him to the stage where one day he may be offered a partnership. If no other suitable employment is to be found the young believer should take the job, but the matter of the future problems which may occur should be made a matter of prayerful consideration. When that day arrives and the offer is made, it will present a lucrative package which appears, on the surface, to guarantee your financial future. At this stage a steady hand and a clear mind is required to discern the real issues at stake. To obey the Master may

A steady hand and a clear mind is required

appear to be turning down so much that is to your benefit, but it will yield great spiritual dividends in the years ahead. The principle taught by the Lord Jesus bears on this situation, " he that loses his life for My sake shall find it" (Mat 16:25).

It must not be thought that the unequal yoke exists only where a written legal agreement is in force. It is perfectly possible for an unequal yoke to exist without any legal agreement in place. If, for instance, you own and run a one-man business, it is possible to have agreements with other business men which constitute the unequal yoke. It is not that every business agreement could be construed in this way, but you may have agreements which limit your actions and which tie you to a common line of practice which may not always be in accord with what you believe. Always be careful that you are not tying yourself into something which will be difficult or even impossible to break.

Be careful that you are not tying yourself into something which will be difficult to break

The unequal yoke in religion

It may seem surprising to speak of the unequal yoke in matters of religion, but there are many opportunities presented to us today which can lead us into such a situation.

Who is in the local church?

The Bible is clear in telling us that a local church is made up of those who are Christians and who have been baptised by immersion as public witness to the change which salvation has brought into their lives. Christians are those who have been saved by acknowledgement of their sin and acceptance of Jesus Christ as their Lord and Saviour. Nowadays there are many religious organisations which have in their ranks those who are not Christians. They may be good-living people who are well intentioned, but they are not believers, and as such we should not be unequally yoked together with them.

A local church is made up of Christians who have been baptised

Should unbelievers be in the local church?

Where it is clear that unbelievers are joining with you, taking part in what is commonly called 'communion' (which is not an expression used in Scripture for the breaking of bread) and participating in the life of the 'church' of which you are a member, this constitutes an unequal yoke.

If you are in such a 'church' you may feel that your position is justified because you are helping to bring the gospel to those who are unbelievers and who are fellow members. You feel, perhaps, that by being there you are able to help keep the church activities on a sounder footing than they would be if you were not there. No doubt your influence is felt, but the presence of those who are not believers severely limits what can be said from the pulpit. It reduces the gospel to a bland message which is designed to offend no

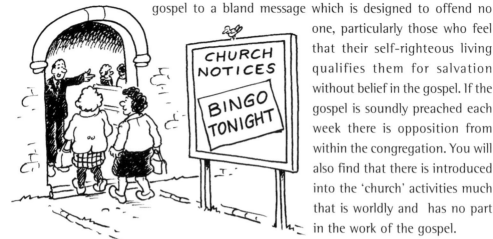

one, particularly those who feel that their self-righteous living qualifies them for salvation without belief in the gospel. If the gospel is soundly preached each week there is opposition from within the congregation. You will also find that there is introduced into the 'church' activities much that is worldly and has no part in the work of the gospel.

Sadly the argument that you are able to bring the gospel to others, does not hold up. But apart from that, you must look at the word of God and see again that you must not be unequally yoked together with unbelievers and, no matter what you feel, or what church background you have, it is never envisaged in Scripture that unbelievers would be associated with the local church.

Better to be working for the Lord Jesus with those who acknowledge Him as their Lord

There are many other issues involved in the Scriptural teaching regarding the local church, but our present subject only covers this one vital area. How much better it would be to be working in testimony for the Lord Jesus with those who acknowledge Him as their Lord and Saviour.

Other associations

We are living in a complex world and many different kinds of associations abound on every hand. Trade associations, unions, charities, clubs of various kinds, and special interests groups are all around us. Some of them seem to have no compromise of truth associated with them and could be most helpful to you. Some are attractive but bring problems with them. Some are necessary if we are to find employment. How, then, does a young believer decide what is and what is not acceptable?

To reach a decision the main question still remains: Does the association involve any compromising of the truth? You must look at every situation and weigh up all the issues. Where compromise is involved you cannot enter into such an association and still make progress in the service of the Master.

When the club or association is purely for spare-time activities consider whether the time and money spent on this would not be better used for the work of the Lord. Remember also the danger of unprofitable social contacts which must be part of the activities of a club. As a broad rule it is wise to join as few organisations as possible, limiting it to those which are necessary and cannot be avoided. Where you feel you must join, be careful to ensure that your freedom to work and testify for the Lord Jesus is not in jeopardy.

It is wise to join as few organisations as possible

Examples from scripture

Eliashib's unequal yoke

"Eliashib the priest, having the oversight of the chamber of the house of our God, was allied unto Tobiah" (Neh 13:4).

We can hardly imagine that one who was High Priest in Israel should enter into an unequal yoke. In Nehemiah 13:4 we find that Eliashib the High Priest is allied to Tobiah, the enemy of Israel. Tobiah was one of the leaders in the opposition to the building of the wall of Jerusalem, and had openly declared his contempt for those who were working under Nehemiah. If we look a little closer we will find that Eliashib's grandson was married to a daughter of Sanballat who was in league with Tobiah. What a strange mixture this seems to be!

No one is immune from failure

We learn from this that no one, no matter how well known in the service of the Lord Jesus, is immune from failure. The High Priest should have been well aware of the dangers in becoming too closely associated with those who were enemies of the God of Israel, but this did not hold him back.

The effect which this had on the life of Israel is clear. In Nehemiah 3 there is the record of the work of the builders as they toiled to build again the broken-down walls of Jerusalem. Right at the beginning of this record we are introduced to Eliashib who is engaged in building the sheep gate. In all, in this chapter, six gates are repaired but you will notice that there is one fundamental difference between the gate which Eliashib built and the others. The sheep gate had no locks and bars on it. Eliashib saw to it that this gate could be closed but not locked. Is this not suggestive of a man who wished to give the impression of being a faithful leader of the people but who wished to be able to compromise when it suited him? It may be that his close friendship with ungodly men allowed him to be put under pressure to leave the gate without locks. He leaves a gate through which he can go when it takes his fancy, and through which outsiders can come whenever they wish. The unequal yoke has led him to a course of compromise which puts Israel at risk.

We see a further evidence of this in Nehemiah 13. During the absence of Nehemiah, the High Priest empties the great chamber in the temple where the sacrifices brought by the people were stored, and prepares it as a home for Tobiah. So the man who left the locks off the gate is now openly welcoming this ungodly man into Jerusalem. To add insult to injury he prepares him lodgings in the temple. Little wonder that this is called "the evil that Eliashib did for Tobiah" (v 7). It falls to Nehemiah to throw all the furniture and goods of Tobiah out of the temple.

> The unequal yoke has led to a course of compromise

It is sad to note that those who enter into unequal links with the world outside may well end up seeking to bring their friends in amongst believers. In Jerusalem the immediate result was that what was provided to store God's offerings and promote His worship was reduced. There was more concern with pleasing the unbeliever than with pleasing God.

Asa's unequal yoke

"Thou hast relied on the king of Syria, and not relied on the Lord thy God" (2 Chron 16:7).

Asa king of Judah was a king who did what was "good and right in the eyes of the Lord his God" (2 Chron 14:2). He was a reformer king who destroyed the altars to strange gods, the images and the high places which had become part of the religious life of Judah. He was determined that all his people would seek the Lord God of their fathers. He fortified the kingdom against invasion by the building of fenced cities, and he was successful in battle. Such was his zeal that when his grandmother made an idol in a grove, he had her removed from her queenly estate.

Baasha king of Israel was his enemy, and when Asa was facing him he entered into an agreement with Ben-hadad king of Syria. He brought the treasure from the house of the Lord and from the king's house and sent them to Ban-hadad as a token of the treaty between them. The king of Syria came to his aid and the king of Israel was defeated. Again this seemed like a very worth-while arrangement which seemed to work out, but it was an unequal yoke.

His unequal yoke placed him on the wrong side

It cost Asa much of his treasure, but it cost him also a great victory which he would have won over the Syrians. The prophet Hanani brought the message to the king that "the king of Syria escaped out of thine hand". Asa has been in treaty with a nation which would be a great enemy of Israel and which he would have conquered if he had remained faithful to the Lord. His unequal yoke placed him on the wrong side.

Jehoshaphat's unequal yoke

"After this did Jehoshaphat king of Judah join himself with Ahaziah king of Israel, who did very wickedly" (2 Chron 20:35).

Jehoshaphat was a very good king of Judah but he had one recurring weakness. On three occasions he linked himself with the godless kings of Israel. He entered into alliance with Ahab (against whom Elijah had prophesied) and with his two sons Ahaziah and Jehoram.

Perhaps he thought he could exert some influence over these godless men to give them desires to live better lives. Whatever his motive, the three kings with whom he allied himself did not change, and Jehoshaphat experienced only anxiety and loss through his associations with them.

The alliance which is mentioned in 2 Chronicles 20 was for commercial purposes. They combined their resources to build a fleet of ships to go to Tarshish, a great commercial centre. This enterprise was doomed to failure, as the Lord intervened and the ships were wrecked before they could reach their destination.

There was really no need of this alliance with a wicked king to increase Jehoshaphat's wealth, for his reign had been very successful commercially. In the cities of Judah there was "much business" transacted (2 Chron 17:13). He was, however, blinded by the possibility of more financial gain, and then found out that the unequal yoke left him very much the poorer.

The unequal yoke left him very much the poorer

Conclusion

The resources which are available to a Christian are immense. God's desire is that we should use these resources and see Him working in our lives. The pressures of modern living make us feel so inadequate at times, and we often forget that there is at our disposal all that is necessary to meet all the challenges of life. Let us never step outside of what God has provided for us.

To enter into an unequal yoke is to declare that God's resources are not adequate for you. That is the pathway to loss. To ensure that all your associations meet with God's approval is the pathway to true and lasting gain.